ROUTLEDGE LIBRARY EDITIONS: HISTORY OF EDUCATION

EDWARD THRING

EDWARD THRING

Maker of Uppingham School
Headmaster 1853 *to* 1887

By

W. F. RAWNSLEY

Volume 27

LONDON AND NEW YORK

First published in 1926
This edition first published in 2007 by
Routledge
2 Park Square, Milton Park, Abingdon, Oxfordshire OX14 4RN
Simultaneously published in the USA and Canada
by Routledge
711 Third Avenue, New York, NY 10017
First issued in paperback 2014

Routledge is an imprint of the Taylor & Francis Group, an informa business

Transferred to Digital Printing 2007

© 2007 Routledge

All rights reserved. No part of this book may be reprinted or reproduced or utilised in any form or by any electronic, mechanical, or other means, now known or hereafter invented, including photocopying and recording, or in any information storage or retrieval system, without permission in writing from the publishers.

British Library Cataloguing in Publication Data
A catalogue record for this book is available from the British Library

Library of Congress Cataloging in Publication Data
A catalog record for this book has been requested

ISBN 978-0-415-43272-6 (hbk)
ISBN 978-0-415-76176-5 (pbk)
ISBN 978-0-415-41978-9 (Set)

Publisher's Note
The publisher has gone to great lengths to ensure the quality of this reprint but points out that some imperfections in the original copies may be apparent.

EDWARD THRING

MAKER OF UPPINGHAM SCHOOL

Headmaster 1853 to 1887

BY

W. F. RAWNSLEY

London:
KEGAN PAUL, TRENCH, TRUBNER & CO., LTD.
Broadway House: 68-74, Carter Lane, E.C.
1926

Printed in Great Britain by
MACKAYS LTD., CHATHAM

The writer of this Article begs to acknowledge the kind permission of Messrs. Macmillan & Co., Ltd., to make use of quotations from Sir G. Parkin's *Life of Ed. Thring* and of Commander O. Locker Lampson, M.P., for permission to use the article on Ed. Thring in the *Empire Review* of Dec., 1924.

EDWARD THRING

EDWARD THRING'S life has been written by Sir George Parkin, to whom Thring took a strong liking, when Parkin, a schoolmaster himself, came to Uppingham in the 'seventies of last century, to get first-hand information about school houses and classes and Thring's own methods of dealing with boys, which had caused him to be considered in the States as the greatest living authority on teaching.

I was then a housemaster, and on Parkin's first appearance, Thring handed him over to me to be shown the plans and arrangements of a typical Uppingham boarding house. He then had some stimulating talks with Thring on all that he most wanted to discuss, and when he re-crossed the Atlantic he plunged at once into matters concerned with education, eventually being promoted to take up the headship of the Upper Canada College at Toronto.

He had come to England at first on a mission in the cause of Empire Federation. All that he spoke for has come to pass, but Thring needed no convincing, he was all for it, and wrote to Parkin : " Your programme is the right one ; more than that, in one form or another it must come to pass."

Subsequently he was chosen to be Organising Secretary of the Rhodes Scholarship Trust, and had to spend a good deal of his time in England. Here he became a devoted friend of Thring, who left him the task of writing his life, so much was he struck by Parkin's breadth of view and the similarity of their ideas on education.

Parkin wrote the book, but as he knew little of Thring's joyous boylike life in the holidays, his merriment and power of throwing aside all care, and putting his whole heart into the fun of the holidays, he had to draw very largely upon the private diaries, in which Thring conscientiously noted down all his difficulties with his masters, all his lifelong trouble to find money to keep things going, and all his secret joys and sorrows—joys happily predominating—in his daily handling of his boys. His boys were always in his mind, and he more than once spoke of his hope and belief that he may have them round him and converse with them as friend to friends, in a future existence; he looked forward to that as his greatest delight.

Anyone who reads these diaries must be greatly struck with the deeply religious nature of the man, who saw God's Hand in all that happened, and whether the happening brought joy or sorrow, was content to accept it and think it best, because he never for a moment mistrusted the Divine leading.

Parkin, even before he became acquainted with these diaries, had written thus: " Edward Thring was unquestionably the most original and striking figure in the schoolmaster world of his time in England; and abroad, he was the only English schoolmaster of the present generation widely and popularly known by name."

His father was Rector of Alford in Somersetshire and squire of the parish. He ruled his family with autocratic severity and lived to be ninety. Mrs Thring, who lived to be over a hundred, was gentle and patient and adored by all her children. Her ancestors had been clergymen for seven generations and her eldest brother, Dr R. Jenkyns, became Master of Balliol.

One of her sons said : " Mother's idea was that everything should be sacrificed to work and duty," and Edward wrote that " a more saintly woman in practice and faith I believe cannot be found."

We can easily see the qualities of both parents reproduced in the son.

His mother, in a letter, tells us that the five boys, two older and two younger than Edward, were always out of doors, but that she did teach four of them to read ; Edward, however, taught himself and learnt the poetry that was set to his elder brothers by listening to them saying it aloud. Also, we gather from the little that has been handed down of his childhood that he was a boy singularly full of energy and with an independent spirit not easily ruled. This occasioned his being sent to a private school in

Ilminster at an early age, where severity and restraint were the leading principles, which rendered, and properly rendered in the opinion of the Headmaster, the young lives with whom he had been entrusted, as miserable as possible.

Thring never forgot those three years of misery; and more than fifty years later, in a public address, he said: "The most lasting lesson of my life was the failure of suspicion and severity to get inside the boy-world, however much it troubled our outsides." And again: "It was my memories of that school which first made me long to try if I could not make the life of small boys at school happier and brighter."

Passing on to Eton in 1832 at the age of eleven, he found a very different school world, with a freedom from restraint which was at first almost embarrassing.

He went first for three years as an Oppidan to the house of Mr Chapman, afterwards Bishop of Colombo, who had married one of the famous Dr Keate's daughters.

Thring always spoke of his housemaster as the kindest of men, and one who tried his best, in the almost impossible circumstances of the time, to do his duty by each boy who came under him; and that being Thring's own great aim and achievement when he became himself a schoolmaster, he always entertained for Chapman the greatest respect and affection.

In 1835 Thring entered College at Eton.

How often in later life have I heard him describe in vivid terms the rough-and-tumble life of " long chamber," an enormous dormitory into which "seventy boys were locked, utterly without supervision, from 8 p.m. until next morning." In one of his writings he speaks of " the wild revelry and fun and the rollicking freedom of that land of misrule, with its strange code of traditional boy-law, which worked rather well, as long as the sixth form were well-disposed and sober. And oh! the unearthly delight of the leaping matches at the end of each school time, when with all the mattresses spread on the hard oak floor to pitch on and one to take off from, the Collegers celebrated their Olympic Games."

Certainly, as another of his contemporaries wrote : " A boy who passed unscathed through

EDWARD THRING

the ordeal of a colleger's life must have been gifted in no common degree with purity of mind and strength of will." And this is exactly what we may safely say that Edward Thring possessed. A pure heart, strength of will, and tremendous energy and a courage which nothing could daunt, were his all through life, and from his earliest days. I believe there is no reason to doubt the story told of him when a small Etonian, that on a big boy threatening to turn him out of the fives court, of which he had obtained priority of possession in the legitimate manner, and asking how he was going to prevent it, he exclaimed, " I'd die first," whence the name of " little die-first " stuck to him for some time. His mother tells us that when, as a new boy at Eton, he was asked to give some evasive answer, he said, " If you want a lie told you must tell it yourself, for I shan't." Though short in stature, he was strong, active and a quite first-rate fives player. He and another Etonian used regularly to play the pick of the school at Uppingham, until he was turned fifty, and generally beat us. I recall one occasion when he sent in a stinger which would have struck the back wall and landed in the pepper-box, but that his partner's head received the ball. We looked for some commiseration, if not apology, but all we heard was: " Why don't you keep your head out of the light ? "

After his three years as an Oppidan, and six at college, he went up to King's in 1841, taking with him about £500, which remained after paying all the expenses of " Montem," the last but one ever held, and at which the salt-bearers, as they were called, had collected about £1,270.

The times were changing, and the advent of the Great Western Railway put an end to the streams of carriages which the boys used to stop and take toll from, on the roads into Eton.

The class lists held no names of King's men in Thring's time. They got their degree without any competition, an anomaly which he worked hard to abolish. But he carried off several college prizes, and had the distinction of winning, in 1845, the Porson prize for Greek Verse, open to the University, and in the same year the Cooke prize, awarded " to those scholars who had deserved well by application to their studies and general orderly behaviour." The idea conveyed in these grandiose terms he perpetuated when Headmaster at Uppingham, by instituting a silver leaving-medal for those in the sixth, inscribed, " For good work and unblemished character."

He tells us that he never enjoyed any time more in his life than the two Longs in which he read at Cambridge. In term time, too, he worked hard, and was soon known as a man of exceptional ability and force of character.

He stayed on at Cambridge three years after taking his degree, and came to the determination of taking Orders, and as he always threw himself heart and soul into everything he took up, he made his life-prayer at this time, and he kept it steadily before him through all his days : " Work till the end of my life, and life till the end of my work."

He now took Orders, and in 1847 obtained a curacy at Gloucester under Mr Hedley, a most exceptionally fine character, who had a powerful influence over him, and it is from this period at Gloucester that, as his biographer says, " his intense religious convictions, the vivid conception of personal relation to God, and the consecration of all his powers to God's service, which afterwards became the ruling motives of his life, seem to have become definitely formed and fixed."

He always recommended the experience to be gained by a clergyman working a parish, as an excellent preparation for a schoolmaster ; and he made no secret of the fact that he learnt his teaching in the National School in his parish of St. James, Gloucester, where as curate he used to take a class.

He worked so hard that he had after a couple of years to take a spell of comparative idleness, and read with private pupils at Marlow, helping in church work there, and in his holidays touring with a brother and one or two friends all over Europe.

A couple of extracts from his diary of 1852 will show how keenly he enjoyed his visit to Italy.

EDWARD THRING

Trieste
October 8th, 1852

Started at six o'clock for Venice by steamer, got in about two, after a beautiful passage. Stayed in Venice that night at Hotel Daniele, which is much abused. Walked about in the evening in the Piazza di San Marco, the most glorious scene imaginable, the Doge's Palace and the sea, the Cathedral and the Piazza itself, filling one's mind with a feeling of dreamy magnificence, more unearthly than anything I had ever felt, as I paced up and down by myself. I could well understand how a native might well feel a want in anything less gorgeous in climate or architecture, however beautiful it might be.

and again :

Assissi
Friday, November 19th

We afterwards went into the Upper Church and saw the works of Cimabue, such as remain. The building itself is very good, a cross with an apse at the end, the model of a church for

EDWARD THRING

our worship. After that, we were shown the refectories, a good *Last Supper* in the small one. The grace used at meals is the same used at King's and some other colleges of Cambridge.

It was at this time of comparative inactivity that I first saw him. His younger brother Godfrey was a curate at Stratfield-Turgis, Hants, close to where the Duke of Wellington lived.

My father was curate at the neighbouring village of Hartley Wespall, where Dr and Mrs Keate and their unmarried daughters lived in the big house not far from the Vicarage. Edward, whenever he came to see Godfrey, used to come on to us, and his visit was always a great delight to all of us. His energy and fun were infectious, and when we moved to Shiplake-on-Thames, he still found his way to us, driving over with Godfrey in a trap with a horse who was a byeword, and pulled the whole sixteen miles like a steam engine. The brothers sat side by side, trusting manfully in Providence, Godfrey with his feet well out, and a rein wrapped twice round each well-gloved hand. Happily the animal was easily steered, and I never heard that they came to grief.

Here at Shiplake they came once on a school-feast day. Thring was delightful, and certainly the school never had such a variety of games or such tremendous ardour exhibited. One game was for a boy, with his hands tied behind him, to grope in a basin of flour with his mouth, for a sixpence. A boy came spluttering out of the flour and proceeded to have a fit. We were anxious, and thought to commiserate the little fellow, but Thring blew him up roundly. "What on earth did he mean by attempting the game if he knew he was liable to fits?" A way of looking at it which quite cured him apparently. It was on these visits that Edward, who loved little children, and was greatly taken by my younger sister, Margaret, whom he called Gretchen, used to bring her the most magnificent toys, such huge boxes of doll's tea-things as we had never dreamt of; and all their lives, long after she had children of her own, they remained the closest and most affectionate of friends.

EDWARD THRING

It was his love of children, as well as his compassion for the boys whose spirits he had seen curbed and deprived of the child's proper heritage of joyous life, that determined him to do what he could to make school a happy place, and even, as he insisted in later years, " a better-than-home place."

After his time in Gloucester and his experience in teaching the small rustics there, a task into which he put his whole soul and all the Thring energy, and where he learnt the fundamental axiom of his Uppingham methods, that it needed the highest teaching skill to take the lowest forms, he had no doubt in his own mind that his profession must be teaching.

He now applied for posts, amongst them for the headmastership of Durham School, which went to Dr Holden, then Headmaster of Uppingham. Thring applied at once for Uppingham, and obtained it in September, 1853. It is to be noted that, as it was then promotion to go from Uppingham to Durham, about fifty years later, when Thring had founded a New Uppingham, the Headmaster of Durham secured promotion by moving thither.

EDWARD THRING

On his very first inspection of Uppingham he told a friend, " I think I have found my life-work to-day."

He never thought of the little old Grammar School as a stepping-stone to some bigger school elsewhere. He knew what he intended to do and he meant to do it *there*. And he brought with him a note-book in which he had entered a full list of all the changes and new methods which he would aim at in his new school, and he never went back from this, but by indomitable pluck and perseverance he actually brought them one and all into being in the first decade and a half of his Headmastership.

My father, who had promised Thring that if he got a school he would send him his boy, took me to Uppingham in April, 1855.

Thring, with his faithful old-English sheep-dog, walked to the station, not then at Uppingham, but three miles off, to meet us ; as we topped the hill from the Welland Valley at Seaton, we saw the church spire, but Archdeacon Johnson's Elizabethan schoolroom, adjoining the church-yard and its rows of limes, was not visible, nor was the old " Hospital," which was the school-house and Thring's home for thirty-four years, and is now the school library ; and at that time there was nothing else belonging to the school.

When Archdeacon Johnson founded the school in 1584, his foundation was for a " Faire Free Grammar School " in each of the market towns of Rutland, Oakham and Uppingham, wich a Headmaster and an Usher, receiving respectively £24 and £12 as a yearly stipend, and a further £6 and £3 for acting as " Warden " and " Subwarden " to the " Hospital " which was attached to each school.

The Hospital provided for the maintenance of fourteen poor men and one poor woman, " to wash their buck clothes,"[1] each pensioner to receive £2, but the one who read the prayers when the Subwarden was absent to receive £4.

When I first entered the school in 1855 it was still called " Uppingham Grammar School," and the school-house was called " The Hospital." Thring was printed on the school list as ' Head-

[1] In *Henry VIII.* Falstaff was put into a " buck basket " with the dirty linen.

master and Warden," and the senior assistant master (the Rev. W. J. Earle) as " Usher and Subwarden."

" The Hospital " was the only school-house, and in this there were thirty-three boarders in my first " half."

We were called at 6.30 summer and winter, and raced down about a furlong through the churchyard to the schoolroom, the door of which was shut not seldom in our breathless faces by the praepostor of the week as the clock struck the last stroke of seven. At this early school Thring, in all his time, was never late, and the Subwarden but once in my time, and as boy and master I spent eighteen happy and useful years there.

These small beginnings will help a reader to understand what a huge task Thring took in hand when he accepted the appointment to Uppingham.

But he had got plans in his head for a right method of education ; and considering that the work was for God, in Whom his trust never failed, he determined to begin at once.

EDWARD THRING

How he got masters to come and spend large sums on building boarding houses, which made the school, and how, in spite of constant urging by his masters, he held tight to the principles of restricted numbers in school and houses, on which he considered that a school ought to be conducted, even though as yet no signs whatever appeared in other schools of these principles being adopted, is part of the unique history of Thring and Uppingham.

When he entered on his Headmastership on September 10th, 1853, all that the Governors furnished from the endowment of about £1,000 a year was a small stipend of £150 to the Headmaster and £130 to his assistant, and they kept the school in repair. The greater part of the money went to provide small exhibitions for boys leaving for Oxford or Cambridge; and a portion was distributed among the Almsmen.

This was all; for, as a younger son, Thring had no fortune of his own.

He found but twenty-five boys. Dr Holden had carried eleven of the younger ones to Durham. There were two masters, one besides the usher;

and for a month the Trustees had left the school to them. A third individual was an entirely inefficient writing-master. He was still at his post when I first entered the school, but I never saw him try to teach anything. He mended quill pens and filled the inkpots and cleared up torn paper. We were always sorry for him; he was so like a poorly-clad character out of Dickens, and I am glad to say, for the honour of Uppingham manners, that no one was ever rude to him.

Thring began his first half with a whole holiday and a cricket match in which he played, as he did for several years either in the school eleven, or against them, for he considered games and athletics to be an important part of school training.

As the numbers grew to 100, 200 and 300, which he had fixed on as the limit, he kept on getting one house built after another; and a schoolroom and chapel built by G. E. Street were added, and the latter, after years of anxious thought and work, was consecrated in April, 1865.

When questioned about his limit of 300, he said : " It is not 300 boys or more that I should be afraid of, it is the masters. Masters for 300 will give me quite trouble enough." On the whole his masters served him far better than his Governors, who preferred the little Grammar School and thwarted him at every turn. With the exception of the Patron, General Johnson, he never had a word of kindness from any of them, though late in the day he found a friend in Sir H. Fludyer. On one audit day, only two days before the chapel was consecrated, he gave the number of the school as 282, and announced the winning of the first Balliol Scholarship and the first Trinity Scholarship at Oxford, and, as he notes in his diary, " not a word from any of them," adding : " A schoolmaster never wants a slave in his Triumphal Car to tell him he is mortal."

I was once talking over an audit of the Governors with Creighton who, as Bishop of Peterborough, was an *ex-officio* member of that body, and he said : " There are several bad governing bodies in England, but none nearly so bad as ours." And he knew what he was talking about.

EDWARD THRING

It was chiefly owing to this that for the first twenty years Thring had to be continually fighting for his principles. Fighting often against his own masters, fighting always against his entirely unsympathetic and often actively opposing body of Governors, the patron being the only one of the whole body who at all understood and believed in him and his work, fighting against the Public School Commissioners, and when he had conquered in his long fierce struggle with them, fighting with the Bishop who had refused to confirm the boys in the school chapel,[1] and finally with the town of Uppingham, who refused on an outbreak of typhoid to put their drains in order ; and rather than yield to them and expose his boys to typhoid, he actually moved the whole school to the coast of Wales and kept the work going there satisfactorily for over a year till the town was only too glad to welcome him and the school back to its proper place.

The principles on which Thring built his school were, that every boy should be taught, and

[1] Bishop Magee, a difficult opponent, but afterwards very friendly.

the stupider the boy, the cleverer should be the teacher who was set to deal with him; that no class should exceed an average of twenty-five boys; also that every boy should have a study which should be "his castle" and his very own. Similarly, that he should have privacy secured to him in the dormitories, and that freedom of friendly access to his form and housemaster should be the rule. Indeed, Thring looked on the part the housemaster's wife played in each house as one of the most humanising influences, and a real part of his system. But the most important thing of all was the inculcation of trust between boys and masters, and of truth in word and deed in all school life. This he called *True Life*, and he was never tired of impressing the absolute necessity of it on us all. In this and in everything he did and said he was always tremendously in earnest and carried us along with him. Thus he raised the tone of the school to a height not as a rule dreamt of by boys, or considered probable by masters. "Only trust the boys and they will rise to trustworthiness" was one of his famous sayings.

EDWARD THRING

Lapses from this pitch of excellence, of course, there were, and then he emptied the vials of his wrath in the strongest terms, not only on the culprits, but upon all who might, he said, if so determined, have prevented the wrong-doing. He looked for this co-operation and didn't look in vain. He had brought from Eton the system of putting much power into the hands of the præpostors and the sixth form, and the responsibility had a steadying effect, so that they used their very considerable authority, as a rule, with wisdom and moderation.

It was this that Mr Gladstone, whom I sat next to at a family dinner-party once at Malwood, when he took occasion to say, "I am a Scot through and through; I have not a drop of blood in my body that is not Scotch," in talking to me of the Eton of his time, called *the System*. He said that Eton in his day "was the greatest pagan school in Christendom, meaning by that, that they taught us no religion." To illustrate this he described to me the preparation for confirmation, if such it could be called, and said that they had a recognised book from which they learnt their lines in chapel. " And yet," he continued, " see what splendid characters it turned out. Of the six above me in school three became bishops, among them Hamilton, Bishop of Salisbury, a saint ; Bishop Selwyn, a hero ; and there were two other clergy who did a splendid work amongst the worst and poorest in the East of London ; and these were not alone. And all of it was due to *the system* ; simply and solely to *the system*." From my Uppingham experience I could quite believe it ; certainly Thring's system of perpetually inculcating the principles of truth, courage and the duty of setting, in all things, a good example, his doctrine in short of " True Life " did make a distinct and lasting mark on his pupils.

How often, when a boy, I have heard him end a school speech with his aspiration that whenever boys went out into the world from Uppingham they would carry with them such rules for conduct and such a determination to live the true life always, that they should get in all lands and among all ranks a character for manliness and upright dealing. This he cared for more by far than for any number of intellectual honours, and he was absolutely sincere about this.

In his Diary of November 18th, 1864, he has this entry :—

"I saw Nettleship off to Oxford this morning, not without prayers on my part. I saw him last night, and told him not to be too anxious ; that life was long and scholarships short, and that in one sense, and that the best, I really did not care whether he won or not, only let him continue to do his best."

And then :—

"Nov. 21st. A great day over—fifty-six boys confirmed, the whole school attended. The Bishop[1] gave a most earnest address to the boys, pressing on them with much power, truths they have heard from us."

"Nov. 25th. To-day, and most unexpectedly by afternoon's post, received the news that Nettleship had got the first Balliol Scholarship, a most pleasant letter from Rawnsley giving me particulars. . . . Recommended Nettleship's

---

[1] Dr Jeune

victory and myself to God." He always lives up to his motto : "*Ora et labora.*"

Then comes the entry :—

"Dec. 8th. For the first time these eleven years, the end of this half-year sees me with no great care, and able in some degree to be at ease. It is a strange feeling ; I keep expecting that something must come. Yet there is much debt still, but the school is so prosperous, and no *draws* now on my income coming, that my heart is fairly at rest, neither is there any childish nonsense amongst the masters any more. The days of nursery rebellions seem past."

These diary extracts let us into the secrets of two of Thring's great troubles during the years that he was building Uppingham, viz., the ever-present and crushing weight of debt, and the difficulty of getting a harmonious set of masters. He had received loans from his family and relatives on starting at Uppingham, and calls or "draws," as he names them, were so constantly, during the earlier years of his Headmastership, being made on him, that he never could get his head above water. In 1859 he writes : "Here

I am after six years of incessant work, head and chief of this school, £3,600 in debt still, and having sunk hundreds and thousands in the cause." A legacy from a cousin brings relief eventually, but not for another fourteen years ; and then not a complete riddance of the millstone about his neck ; and he died a poor man.

The trouble with the masters was, as we noted above, lessening at the end of 1864, but nine years later he is again " full of masters' quarrels."

Under the date Nov. 12th, 1873, he writes in his diary :—

" How strangely different the world I live in now, from the world I started to live in ! How painfully different! Then it was full of education and teaching, and the boys, and what was good for them. My school work was all in all ; now I am full of masters' quarrels, and my time and brain is absorbed in tomfoolery ; and I don't see how to escape from it."

In the following year he almost despairs and has little hope that his work will not be undone in a very few years by masters and trustees. But things at their worst improve ; and when, in spite of all kinds of opposition on the part of the Trustees, who wished to keep the school to its original Grammar School size and purpose, and actually propounded a scheme for this to the Commissioners without any consultation with Thring, the first meeting of the Trustees under the new scheme was held on August 17th, 1875, the Headmaster found that he " had friends to deal with instead of opponents," and in his diary he exclaims in his favourite Biblical language : " When the Lord turned again the captivity of Zion, then were we like unto them that dream " ; twenty years of fog and cloud and cold were rolling away.

Thring's plan was to put the boy-life and its good first. The master would find his reward in doing good work ; but unless he could take the view that there was no derogation in being put to take a low class, Thring candidly told each applicant for a mastership that his place was not at Uppingham. To him a low class was not low work ; quite the reverse. " The worse the material, the greater the skill of the worker."

But he always left a good worker to work in

EDWARD THRING

his own way, a thing which greatly enhanced the pleasure we felt in doing the work he wanted.

He made only two stipulations when I became a Housemaster which were thus expressed in a brief note :

"You can poison yourself with whom you please, but for the boys you must employ the school doctor. And the beer you give the boys must be of good strength and quality."

Thring was not quarrelsome. He followed the advice of Polonius in *Hamlet*:

> " Beware of entrance to a quarrel ; but, being in,
> Bear't that the opposed may beware of thee."

From his earliest Eton days he was indeed a fighter, not that he loved fighting ; peace and quiet was his constant prayer ; but when it came to an attack on his principles of Education he would fight literally to the death in the full assurance that thus he was doing the work assigned to him by God.

His one steadfast friend among the Governors, General Johnson, the Patron, writes to him in 1859 to assure him that he will back him to the best of his powers, but warns him not to expect much, as " some of the Governors, he fears, have not the prosperity of the school at heart." Thring's note to this is : " I know that, but we shall ride over them in time if they won't move on."

In the very next year Thring is consulted about the founding of Clifton College and his diary says : " After much talk with Mr Warborough of Bristol I think they will found a really fine school on our system." The next entry in his diary is : " Could not help feeling bitterly, as I was writing to-day about the proposed Bristol scheme, at the zeal and liberality there, contrasted with everything mean, petty and obstructive here, the Governors setting the example which has been well followed."

His system and the visible results were recognised fully in Bristol. His mother writes to tell him that she hears from the Bishop that the Bristol people are going to adopt the Uppingham system as the best of all the public schools. That his father should hear this is, he says, a ray of sunshine to him.

EDWARD THRING

Having received the report from Clifton College for review, he took the opportunity of letting the Patron see it, and the General took good care, as it was not marked private, that the Governor should see it, and possibly begin to understand what others thought of the work they had so constantly opposed at Uppingham.

The move succeeded beyond his hopes, and after foiling, like a massive wall, his every effort as far as they could for seven long years, he writes on November 30th, 1860 :

"This night I stand victorious at the top of the breach. To-day they have decided on building our schoolroom, submitting the plans for our approval before they are carried out."

This last stipulation was one for which he would fight for ever. He would rather have no schoolroom than put up an inferior building. With him, for boys and for education, the best was but just good enough. The Governors were quite ready to have a first-rate man, but because Thring had selected G. E. Street and got plans from him, they determined to have somebody else, and asked Scott to do it. "He repudiated," says the diary, " in the handsomest manner the idea of taking work out of Street's hands and snubbed the Governors soundly for their behaviour in thinking of it."

It was in 1861 that his old Eton friend, Witts, joined him as a master and at once set about building a fine house (Highfield) and started the chapel fund with a subscription of a thousand pounds.

The October diary here speaks of the hearty assistance given him by Dr Acland. " He was the first public man who gave me a cheering word here ; I shall not forget that as long as I remember anything. Rawnsley was the first man who sent his son, and dear old Newbolt the first family neighbour who announced his intention of backing me by sending his."[1]

The growth of the school for the first four years was very slow, and after that it was a matter of general rejoicing when an entry of a dozen boys was made. But Thring was all the time preparing for the influx which he felt sure

[1] This son was the present Canon Newbolt, Chancellor of St. Paul's.

of from the beginning, and so, as the sites of three public houses came one by one into the market, he strained every nerve to raise money and buy the land and the buildings on it in order to have room to build the chapel and schoolroom on which he had fixed his mind, and sites for masters' houses which the increased entries would require ; all he had, even when I first entered the school, being his own school-house, which in the days of his pre-predecessor, when boys slept three in a bed,[1] was ample for his 101 boys, over forty of whom must have been day-boys, but under Dr Holden and still more under his own system of not only a separate bed, but a separate cubicle for each boy, only held thirty-three. Three or four more had their meals at the school-house, and a separate room for a study between them. They slept near at hand

[1] That boys slept three in a bed is not an invention of mine, but was told me by an old woman who lived in the School lane, and had acted as bed-maker in Dr Butterton's time. She also described the appalling noise made in the dormitories on the last morning of term, when all the boys lifted their heavy oak bedsteads at the foot and then, at a given signal, let them all drop. They had special names both for the ceremony and the noise. But I am afraid there is no authentic record of this nor anyone now living who could enlighten us.

in what was called "the Lodge." The School Quad had some twenty-four little studies on two sides of it, like little cloister cells, but very comfortable.

Obviously, until houses could be built the school could not expand even if the entries did. Here was where Thring's indomitable courage came in. He guaranteed the masters a decent salary until they had a house and boys enough to bring them in a living, and he borrowed on bond and mortgage large sums for purchase of the sites as they came into the market, and when, after the first two years, there came a master, the Rev. R. J. Hodgkinson, who had the means, and, caught by Thring's infectious enthusiasm, was ready to spend his patrimony in the venture, the vision of the building of Uppingham School became a tangible fact, and year after year, master after master saw that it was well worth his while to lay out money on building a house which the increasing popularity of the school was bound to fill as fast as each house was ready.

We boys now began to hear of " Thring and

Uppingham," whereas previously nothing used to annoy us more than to be asked where we were at school, and when we said " at Uppingham " to hear the invariable rejoinder, " Uppingham ? Where's that ? "

Things were beginning to go, between 1855 and 1860, when a sort of blight fell on us in 1861 in a most unexpected manner. We used to have only two " halves " with Midsummer and Christmas holidays. But to ease these long halves we had three days at Michaelmas, when only boys who had friends near went away ; but, for the rest, each day was a time of perfect liberty and the Headmaster and his wife joined the boys in providing some entertainment in the evenings. At Easter the holiday was a week or rather more, and few boys remained at the school ; but as it was well known that boys would be inclined, and their parents, too, to stretch the short holiday out, Thring gave out that any boy who failed to return on the proper day would render himself liable to a flogging, *i.e.*, a caning; a birch, though figuring on the Elizabethan seal of the school, was never seen at Uppingham.

EDWARD THRING

Two boys went to spend the time with their grandmother and easily persuaded her that a day or so more of Easter holiday was not at all an uncommon thing, so they returned late and received the reward as advertised. I was present as the culprits left the Headmaster's classroom and heard them say with some sort of glee: " Well ! that did not hurt much." They had but received four strokes. But their weak father chose to take it ill, though the boys themselves had never dreamt of complaining, and, urged by some probably well-meaning, but certainly ill-informed, friends, he wrote furious letters to Thring ; and the papers, scenting blood, took up the case with extraordinary virulence. It is true that the boys were older than their stature and intelligence would indicate. The " Jackson row " did not easily cease. Thring notes that " it has assumed gigantic proportions " by the following year, and that he is " honoured with scurrilous notices in sundry of the low papers and private letters of the most violent abuse. " Some harm, I think it will do, but I think some good also. I may truly say in this matter "God is on my side, I will not fear what man can do unto me."

That the *Saturday Review* should have written a sarcastic satire on him gave him real pain ; not only for the personal attack but for the harm it might do to education generally. He ends his note of this fact by " However, I defy the Devil and all his works."

Punch, he says, was more sensible, and it was certainly more amusing when it said that " Mr Thring seemed to know how to manage boys, and if he did not train their minds he made them mind their trains." It was all a storm in a teacup, but it did a good deal of harm. For a time the entries entirely stopped, and Thring was accused repeatedly of undue severity, which was never true of him, and for the next two years the entries were obviously affected by it. He was ever vigilant and was determined that no real evil should creep into his school and he was able to say about this time " The school is now wonderfully clear of direct evil. There is now not one bad boy here of any age."

I would make my own comment on this remarkable statement, which is, that Thring, in limiting the number of boys he would take, besides his dread of too many masters, had made up his mind that to influence boys a master must *know* them and they must feel that they are known ; and he *did* know all his boys in a truly wonderful manner and was never afraid of talking with them, and to his great delight he was constantly finding that they would of their own initiative come to his study and lay their difficulties or their shortcomings before him and claim his sympathy. These talks, which we called " paternals," always had a marked effect for good.

I have before me now a letter from a parent who knew the school very thoroughly, in which he says : " Thring was the only man alive in his time who combined the strong governing power of a great Headmaster with the faculty of a thorough sympathy with boys' nature which he showed so abundantly in the holidays and out of school and which induced at all times the strong affection of his pupils." He felt strongly, as that great educationist, Miss Charlotte Mason, did, that children should be dealt with as individuals and not in masses.

This incredible row about nothing having in time died out, Thring turned his attention to raising the money needed for the schoolroom and not without what he calls " a sharp encounter " with the Governors, one of whom had the effrontery to tell him that his venture at Uppingham was " nothing but a money speculation." His answer was a dignified one, that " he believed in education and in the greatness of the work he had undertaken in order to supply education in a country which was so much in need of it. That he was ready from the beginning to stake his life on it and was ready still, but now things were improved and even if he was ruined, there were those gone forth who would never forget the system they had been under. The seed was sown and he had no further anxiety about that. There had been all along no hope to make money, but an anxious desire to serve God." Two months later the schoolroom was opened on June 18th, 1862. The governors had given the site and the masters had paid for the building, which they then presented to the Trust. Thring made on this occasion one of his stirring speeches to the school. He told them that the story of their life was very simple. "An earnest desire to work out truth and faith in truth against any odds; a belief that the young need not be false—that is all. We have had ten years of laborious commonplace days, and now you have a desire to claim a position among English schools; now, you cannot *claim* it. It must come. Increase of numbers or mere identity with other schools are not things which have made us what we are. Yet be sure there is the means here of being great. Have you so soon forgotten the motto in your sixth form room :

> 'Self-reverence, self-knowledge, self-control,
> These three alone lead life to sovereign power.'

Yes, power must come, but there are two ways for it to come. Most of all and first, the winning a character for truth and true honour. No lie in word or deed, no sham, no underhand deceits shall harbour here, nothing that will not bear the light. Let this be the school character, as I

EDWARD THRING

trust it is, and fear not the school *is* great. Secondly, power can come by winning a character for scholarship. For this there must be true untiring work and an appreciation of work and a caring for the renown of scholarship; and until this feeling is universal no school will reach its full stature. Be then great, and fill out with daily growing power this temple of learning in which we are to-day. Who shall set a limit to the power that goes forth from here? It will grow and grow and be a witness in all lands . . . And in years to come when men think of their youth and talk one with another of truth and honour and steadfast work, the name of the school shall rise readily to their lips, and deeds of patient endurance, and character, hardly won, for quiet trustworthiness shall fill with honest pride the hearts of those who then will be able to say ' and I, too, was at Uppingham.' Nothing is too great for the power of truth."

This was the kind of speech Thring made to us whenever an occasion for a speech arose, and his tremendous earnestness and the appeal in his voice and the knowledge we all had that he meant every word he said, made us all disciples right through the school, and whilst we admired his courage and feared his wrath, we warmed to his patriotic appeal, believed in his absolute truthfulness and justice, and felt for him, everyone of us, an admiration and an affection to an extent which I doubt if any other headmaster ever evoked.

It was curious, and to Thring a most uplifting thing, that these words of his, the tenor of which so constantly kept ringing in our ears, were shown a very few years later to be a prophecy fulfilled. The Governor of the North-West Provinces of India, Sir George Couper, who had a son at Uppingham, hearing that an Indian Civil Servant had spoken disparagingly of Thring and his school, sent for him and told him that to use the language he had done was to declare himself a renegade, and he had better say nothing in future against Uppingham, whose sons had already made themselves a name for truth and honour and good work in many ways and many places throughout India.

The schoolroom being opened, the next great labour was the chapel. This Thring would have liked to have opened first. His whole life was one of earnest prayer, and no one who knew him could for a moment look upon the frequent expressions of religious feeling in his diary, as in the least degree unreal. He lived in an atmosphere of faith and prayer, just like the patriarchs of old ; and, as James Lonsdale wrote of him, " he seemed to see God with his eye."

He was no humbug and did not let his feeling of the nearness of God obtrude itself in the ordinary affairs of life. One of his maxims was " Nothing is more fatal in a school than obtrusive religion." He declined the offer of a Divinity prize and stated his belief that a school could easily have too many prizes and scholarships, but he willingly lowered the terms for a good needy boy if he could do so at his own expense and not at that of another master. Always, from his curate days, he looked on religion as a very integral part of education, and fine buildings and all that made a worthy setting for worship he made a great point of. When I first entered we used to go to the Parish Church and sit in a gallery at the east end of the south aisle. We were all packed together on narrow deal benches and close to the roof, but we were just opposite to Jeremy Taylor's old pulpit and should have heard the words of the service and the sermon well, but the Rector, a dear old kindly man, had no teeth, and not a single word could we hear. As we outgrew this little gallery we managed to have an afternoon service to ourselves conducted by the masters, from some of whom we heard most excellent sermons. Still we felt like aliens in the Parish Church, and a school chapel was urgently wanted to put the proper religious tone into our Sundays and particularly for our Confirmations. In these early days Thring always gave us a short sermon at Sunday evening prayers in the schoolroom hall, and they were strikingly and admirably adapted to make a deep impression on his hearers. He published them, 47 in number, in 1858. I used to read one each Sunday evening in my house (Fircroft), and I know of none better.

Nothing could be more solemn or impressive than Thring's preparation of Confirmation candidates, but we had to go by rail to Peterborough, lunch at the station restaurant and walk through the town to the Cathedral, where the aged Bishop Davys, Queen Victoria's first tutor, as good and wise a man as ever lived, confirmed us, and then there was all the journey home, and, though Thring himself accompanied us, the ceremony was drowned in the ordinary feeling of an outing to Peterborough. At length the Parish Church was to be " restored " and no longer able to be used for service. We then had Service in the School-house dining-hall, which was most inconveniently crowded, and Thring himself was rather taken aback when on giving out the text of his sermon he found himself saying " And the house of Baal was full from one end to another."

Of course, the school having its own chapel made an enormous difference. The building itself was the centre of the religious life of the boys and seemed part of their education. There was difficulty in getting the contract taken, and when this was arranged the excellent Clerk of the Works was very strict, making the builders take down several feet of wall in one place to get out a stone which had been laid not as it had lain in its original bed, and again when it came to the roof, carefully inspecting every bit of timber, until the road to Leicester was crowded with timber waggons taking back the rejected material. Another exposure of the methods of contractors was made when the Cumberland slates were put on the schoolroom roof and, when all were affixed to the wooden boarding, a space as big as a cricket-pitch was left bare of slate. Thring pointed this out to me and said " that represents the amount the contractor meant to crib by not making the slates overlap as much as the architect required."

This strictness of supervision broke the contractor, and he had to give it up, and the whole work, finished to the wall-plate, but roofless, came to a standstill until more than a year later another was found to tender for the work. It was a splendid piece of work all through when completed ; and when Mr Street was congratulated on it he said : " Yes, you let me build a good wall, Mr Thring." That was the secret of its excellence, Thring's first principle in all good work being to get a really good man and give him perfect freedom. Interference from outside with the skilled workman in his own work, whether of construction or of teaching, was what he fought against so stoutly both with the Governors and also with the Public School Commission.

The chapel was finished and consecrated on April 27th, 1865. And before we speak fully of the struggle which Thring had for the next seven years with the School Commissioners, we may as well note what had been accomplished by him during the past fifteen years.

He had raised the status of the school from a little county Grammar School to an acknowledged position among the best of the English Public Schools. His twenty-five pupils had become three hundred. Boarding houses to accommodate them had been put up, a noble chapel had been built as a centre of the common religious life of the school, and a schoolroom large enough to hold all the boys. A Lower School had been provided and a school hospital, and all the equipment for the games usual in Public Schools had been secured, and several features, now in general use, but before Thring's time unknown in schools, had been added. These were a swimming-bath, a gymnasium, and a carpenter's and metal shop with competent instructors. The first school mission, either home or foreign, had also been started with excellent results, on a plan that all schools speedily adopted. To these, later, were added the school gardens and aviary. The principle that something should be provided to interest boys who might not find the ordinary school curriculum or games sufficiently absorbing was one of Thring's axioms in training ; his desire being to provide something for each individual boy to take hold of. This was his main reason for playing not fives only, but cricket and football with the boys, whilst he was able ; a word of praise for skill or pluck in games being a real help to a boy who had never been able to win any positive commendations in class. Moreover, the games and athletics had an important effect, he considered, on a boy's character, while to endure defeat bravely was in itself a victory.

Accordingly, his principle of getting for all school work the best possible master and giving him his head, was carried out in games as in work and made the school so famous in the seventies for its cricket that in one year no fewer than five Uppinghamians were playing for Cambridge in the University match ; for Thring, through C. E. Green, had secured for the school that prince of professionals, H. H. Stephenson, and given him, on the field, the status of a recognized master.

The Cambridge players in 1877 were

   W. S. Patterson,
   A. P. Lucas,
   D. Q. Steel,
   H. T. Luddington,
   S. S. Schultz.

H. H. Stephenson came to the School in 1872 and served it right well for twenty-five years. And here I will quote from W. S. Patersons' *Sixty Years of Uppingham Cricket.*

"It was in May, 1872, and Haileybury had come over to play at Uppingham. The school got a very big score, 374, of which W. S. Patterson got 116. In Thring's diary we read :

May 28th. To-day the Haileybury match. The poor Haileybury team had us in first, and we got over 370 runs, and they have six wickets down for 25 or so. I am sorry for it. They are a very nice set of fellows and it will so spoil their outing. Moreover, I don't want the cricket to get too powerful in the school here—and to be worshipped and made the end of life for a considerable section of the school.

(A characteristic entry of the dear old Head.)"

In April, 1869, the school started its first East End Mission (its previous contributions being sent annually to Brisbane, Australia), and for many years it paid £150 annually to carry on the work in a district selected by the Bishop of London. An old boy, Wynford Alington, uncle of the present Headmaster of Eton, was missioner under the Rev. Dr Boyd, late principal of Hertford College, Oxford, at North Woolwich; and Thring once took a select company of the boys and an efficient choir to London and housed them there, and took them to a service at North Woolwich next day, to celebrate the opening of a new church there; seventy-four went from Uppingham and fifteen old boys joined them. This visit was not the only one, and Dr Boyd wrote years afterwards : " My feeling of gratitude to the school for the help and sympathy it gave me so cordially when I was hard pressed in London, but deepens as the years go on."

The Mission went later to Poplar, and the choir and music-master and some of the ladies gave concerts there occasionally on behalf of the poor.

It seemed to Thring to be "a great thing to put the idea into the boys of giving personal help to the poor." He was proud, too, to have " started a thing likely to be imitated and to bear good fruit," as indeed it has.

Another thing which the public schools have not all been able to copy was his insistency that in every house each boy should have a study to himself, and his own cubicle for privacy in every dormitory. This was a great boon.

Then, to his everlasting credit, for he was not in any sense musical himself, he had put the teaching of music on a firm basis by securing the best possible teachers and giving the boys concerts with first-rate music only, which he plainly saw had a refining and elevating influence in school training, and, here too, according to his custom, having secured the best of teachers, he gave them an absolutely free hand. And the results which Herr David produced during his long service at Uppingham made the school famous for its music and its concerts, as it still continues to be.

The delight with which Thring welcomed Joachim who used to visit David, and rejoiced in the boys' singing and was never tired of playing to them ; this and the playing of many other distinguished musicians such as Piatti and Ludwig and Ferdinand Hiller, whilst Sterndale Bennett and Sir Charles Villiers Stanford paid us frequent visits, only increased Thring's sympathy and admiration for the school's music, and he composed the school songs, which David set and which have become a precious school heritage.

He had been very fortunate in getting as teacher what he asked for, viz., " a first-rate musician who has made music his profession and is a master in it, and withal a man of personal powers and go, who can inspirit the boys, and breathe some enthusiasm into them." Having got the right man, he made singing-practice compulsory, and subject to the same discipline as the regular school classes, and himself frequently attended at the practices, especially those on Sunday evenings, and, hating dilettantism, he was pleased to find how eagerly the boys took to the study of the best classical music. Next to himself there was no more popular Master than Herr David, and the outward and visible sign of this is the fine *David Memorial Hall* put up in Dr Selwyn's time as a gymnasium and school concert hall.

The school concerts were for many years called " drawing-room evenings," because Thring and Mrs Thring, believing in the potency of music, at a time when there was no adequate room to hold the performers and no school-house except their own, used twice every half to ask all the boys to tea, followed by music in their drawing-room, now the masters' common room. We dressed for it, and boys with voices were selected for solo, trio, or quartette, and a lady would sing or play, and for the time we were just one big family. Thring's school songs had not then been written, but everyone joined heartily in choruses, which our sole music-master, Herr Schafer, conducted. Such was the beginning of the fine music for which our dear old friend Paul David made Uppingham famous.

The changing of boys' voices and the breaking of the voice make a choirmaster's task at a school a difficult one, and the fact that the whole generation of boys passes away in about three years necessitates a constant repetition of the same work, and we know that

"*occidit miserum crambe repetita magistrum.*"

But for all that, how much has been accomplished for many years at Uppingham, as it has at Cranleigh School, by the constant efforts of a real musician spread over forty years!

Besides his encouragement of good music, Thring did what he could to give boys a taste for good painting, and with the boys of the schoolhouse, would at times in his drawing-room go through a large portfolio of photographs of the world-famous pictures of the great masters, with information about their lives, thus opening new interests and pleasures to many a boy.

Also on wet afternoons he invited all who liked to come to the School-house Hall, where he gave a demonstration of the working of an air-pump and an electric machine. Physics were supposed to be taught by the German master, whose German pupils were very few, and there were two French masters, but I once heard an " old boy " say at a big Uppingham meeting, " Thring knew what he could do and what he couldn't. He never tried to teach us French " ; and, indeed, at the time it was taught in most schools, but very little learnt. James Lonsdale once told me that at Eton, when the French master had made a pathetic appeal to his class after the letting loose of a sparrow in class with the natural consequences, and the boys were moved by his appeal, he spoilt it all by referring to the sparrow as " zat fowl."

A Public School Commission had been appointed in 1865, and Thring knew that he would have to fight hard for every one of the principles on which he was building up his school. He had been received by the Commissioners in a quite friendly manner, and hoped to find some at least of his views embodied in their Report, but when it appeared they were not even referred to. On this he says : " How ridiculous it will seem in years to come appointing a lot of squires and a stray Lord or two to gather promiscuous evidence on an intricate professional question and sum up and pronounce infallible judgment on it. But that is the English panacea now." He felt this Report to be " The heaviest possible blow to education, and the most unexpected reverse that the cause of the work has received or can receive."

He told Mr Roby, the Secretary, that he wished, in every way he could, to help and not to oppose, believing that the Commission wished much good to education, but he knew that Archdeacon Johnson's was distinctly a Church foundation, and if they were going to alter this, either the Government must give them back their chapel and schoolroom and let them start for themselves, or else he would place his resignation in their hands and they must restart the school without him.

His present school had arisen in the faith that the original foundation was of a Church of

England character and as such he demanded that it should now be recognised.

Lord Lyttelton told Thring that he could not see that Uppingham could obtain different treatment from that accorded to other schools, upon which Thring pointed out that the men who had contributed to the refounding of Uppingham were still alive ; that the work had all been done in one generation, and that these facts made the case of Uppingham peculiar among foundation schools. But when the draft scheme for the school came down, it proved to be as bad as possible, and he could only tell the masters that there were three or four points in it on which there could be no giving way, and even no compromise.

As a matter of fact, the scheme proposed to leave the school in the hands and under the management of the old body of Governors, who had contributed less than nine per cent. of the expense of the school buildings, Thring and his masters finding the other ninety-one per cent.

The unfairness of this was so striking that two of Thring's strongest supporters, Mr Jacob of Liverpool and Mr Birley of Manchester, from which two towns a large number of boys came to Uppingham, told one of the Commissioners if they forced Thring to resign they would carry off the boys and found Uppingham anew elsewhere, leaving them only the empty walls. On one occasion " Lyttelton asked if Thring would persist in refusing to accept the scheme, even if he was not one of the exceptions provided in the Bill. ' Certainly we should,' " I said. He said, " But that is like running your head against a wall." " Exactly what we mean to do," I answered, " if necessary." After this, when the position of the masters in regard to their houses at Rugby was mentioned, Canon Robinson neatly summarised the case by saying : " I see, at Rugby the school made the houses, at Uppingham the houses make the school." " Exactly so," I said ; " that represents the pivot of the thing completely."

Another strong point was made by Thring, distinguishing between supervision, which he admitted, and interference and power of initiating and prescribing, which he said nothing should ever induce him to work under.

After this the obnoxious clauses were all modified, and the chief points for which he contended were embodied in the constitution of the school.

"If ever," says Parkin, "man had a right to reap the practical fruits of success, Thring had. But what cheered him most was to feel that the strong stand he had made for Uppingham would make the future safer for other schools." His determined resistance to the proposals of the Public Schools Commission brought him a well-deserved victory. The Church character of the school was maintained. The masters received due representation on the governing body, and the internal management of the school, instead of being given over to amateur rulers, remained in the hands of the Headmaster and his staff, "the skilled workers."

One of his great achievements was the setting up of the Headmasters' Conference. In doing this he had a strong coadjutor in Harper, the Headmaster of Sherborne.

It was whilst the Endowed Schools Bill was before Parliament that Bishop Mitchinson, Headmaster of Canterbury, invited several of his brother Headmasters to meet and discuss it, at the Freemasons' Tavern in London. Twenty-five or six attended, and after a good discussion, they passed a resolution to interview Forster, the Vice-President of the Council. Before the close of the second meeting, Thring rose and, after speaking of the use and pleasantness of such a meeting as they had held, proposed that they should make it an annual custom to meet together, and invited all who were willing to meet next Christmas at Uppingham. This was the first Headmasters' Conference, the date being 1869.

Of sixty to seventy invitations, the answer in most cases and for various reasons very courteously expressed was : " I pray thee have me excused." Twelve came. There is this note in his November diary : " A rather impudent letter this morning in answer to my Congress invitation. It is amusing to see how exactly those schools that are most rotten stand on their hindlegs."

Thring wished to get the skilled workmen together, because he thought that their skill was lying, like the seed in the parable, scattered by the wayside for the birds of the air to peck at and devour, and for amateur authorities to trample underfoot. They wanted union.

This he told to the " lady teachers of England " when he had invited the London Society of Schoolmistresses to hold their annual Conference in June, 1887, at Uppingham, where they had a most happy meeting under his genial leadership. " Fifty-nine came, and we did all in our power to honour them . . . and a very remarkable set of able and interesting women they were," says the diary, and again, " These two most important days come and gone . . . the ladies exceedingly gratified, and our own masters and the school ladies, I believe, quite as much so. The conversazione and the music were perfect." Thring ended an impressive address to them with the words, " The hope of teaching lies in you." Miss Buss, the President, sending a beautiful edition of Ruskin's works as a memento of the visit, writes thus : " We who have worked so long and aspired so constantly to raise girls' education to a higher level, have often felt the need of more direct encouragement, and a further faith in our endeavour, on the part of men engaged on similar work." And in truth, this Uppingham visit was the first occasion on which such hearty recognition had been given by any educational authority to women workers in the same great cause, and marked the beginning of a new epoch.

Miss Beale, of Cheltenham, also wrote in the warmest terms: " No school has ever impressed me like Uppingham; other schools may be bodies corporate, but Uppingham has a soul." With these distinguished teachers, as also with Mrs Charles Kingsley and Mrs Ewing, Thring formed a close and lasting friendship. It is one mark of Thring's true greatness, that those whose good opinion was best worth having, always greatly esteemed him. Pope in a letter to Swift says: " Great geniuses must and do esteem one another, and I question if any others can esteem or comprehend uncommon merit," and Addington Symonds strikes the same note when he says: " Nothing is more difficult than for lesser men or equals to pay just homage to the greatest, in their life-time." The friendly intercourse and the interchange of views among even a few educated men was, of course, a pleasure ; and the numbers of those who came to the Headmasters' Conference increased every time. The meeting was held at a different school each year, and the tenth is thus described in Thring's diary for 1879. " The Conference at Eton was a great success in putting the finishing stroke to its power and importance. We were, of course, received very sumptuously. . . . It was a very striking fact, some 140 head and assistant masters meeting at Eton, and marks a memorable epoch." This Conference has been established now for over fifty years, and is still going strong. It is interesting to see how Etonian Thring was. Someone at the first Conference proposed that they should ask the Headmaster of Eton to be their President. Thring objected, as he thought they ought to meet at a different school each time when possible, and that the Headmaster of that school ought naturally to preside, and in a strong speech he said : " I cannot be suspected of not appreciating the great schools ; I was nine years at Eton, I am a King's man, and examiner at Eton for four consecutive years for the election to King's, and am thoroughly sensible of the wonderful advantages of my old school, I speak of Eton as the one I am best acquainted with, and take it as a type ; but our cause, I conceive, is in one sense quite distinct from that of the great schools. We take our stand on work and living progress, and invite co-operation. To me Eton seems the perfection of a school in external advantages, a fairyland (I speak with no disrespect to others), and it has wonderful power of a certain kind, and earnest men using that power . . . We wish to keep our arms open to receive adherents from all schools, being always ready to give a friendly reception to a newcomer, whether he come early or late. The great schools, I can say, have been exceedingly courteous, in all communications that have passed : I trust they will be willing to take our ground of thorough true life and progress, as their ground, and meet us on it."

Thring had by this time made a great mark, and letters kept coming to him from far overseas, from Canada and from Australia as well as from India, saying how strongly his school was recommended and what a high character the men he had turned out had gained.

He knew now that he had succeeded in his main object, and that the boys he had trained were carrying out the high ideals for which he had aimed and fought. He always made a great distinction between teaching and training. It was the latter that entitled him to insist on a good school being " a better-than-home place." Parents might get teaching for their boys done at home, but not training ; and that was the priceless outcome of life at school, if the school really taught and guided every boy in it ; and we have seen that that was his first aim at Uppingham.

The teaching was often open to criticism ; but the teaching and training combined produced a really excellent result. This will, perhaps, be better understood if we look at some of the correspondence between the pupils and their old Headmaster. His influence was far from ending with the close of a school career, and how powerful it was may be judged from the delight of his pupils to welcome his short visits to Oxford or

EDWARD THRING

Cambridge, and from the way they had when any question of right or wrong had to be decided, of asking not " what would my father say ? " for then the answer was not always clear and certain, but " what would Thring say ? " and the answer was clear at once.

His correspondence with his old boys took up much of his time, but was a great delight to him. The following few quotations are from his letters to and from his most distinguished pupil, R. L. Nettleship. Thring had noted from the very first, when Nettleship was a new boy, " This boy will go far." After he had gained his Balliol scholarship he wrote in 1864 : " I congratulate you heartily, and it would be affectation to deny that your success is of great importance to me and the school, but you know my feelings. I look onwards, and real work is real work, whether defeated or victorious . . ."

Similar congratulations on his winning the *Hertford* and the *Ireland* scholarships followed in 1866 and 1867. And in order to share his pleasure with the boys, Thring " walked into afternoon school " (he seldom took a class in the

EDWARD THRING

afternoon himself) " and let all the classes out; so a halo of satisfaction settled on the afternoon."

In 1869 Nettleship wrote to him : " I have been asked to ask you to prolong the Easter holidays to ten days, for the *Jenkyns*. For myself I see no reason why you should, nor do I know precisely on what principle you go in these matters, much less how far the extension of the holidays is bad or good as a bit of school administration ; however, I feel very strongly that any success of mine belongs to you and the school, and especially to you in the present instance, so I should be very glad if you thought this a good opportunity of showing it. I will not say much about your last letter, only this, that it came to me like a blast of a trumpet, breathing strength and courage."

Four months later Thring wrote to him about his future work : " You have just anticipated what I was going to suggest. In the visiting amongst the poor there is an absolute necessity, if you are to carry out your great work worthily, that you should lay your foundations deep in the great realities of life, and that can only be by learning the sufferings and glories of the poor."

The next letter from Nettleship began: "I have got a second. As far as I am concerned, it does not matter a straw. But I am sorry for the school and you. It would have given a completeness to it all to be able to say I had got a first." Thring's rejoinder begins: "You know very little of me if you think I care for your second class. Hang the completeness." To his brother Godfrey, he says, as his Diary often reiterates: "I go so far as to think that what seems mistaken is very often, when honestly done, most blessed, and our misfortunes are our greatest gains." The lost battle he was able often to look upon as a real victory.

He had meant to do his life's work at Uppingham, and could not be tempted to leave it, though he had the offer of at least one famous public school, and was glad because it pleased his parents. They were a remarkable couple. The father, autocratic, and not fond of contradiction, was more the Squire than the Parson, and Edward, even after taking Orders, was always called by the keeper at Alford "the Young Squire." Indeed, he had inherited all the tastes of a country gentleman, and was no mere pedagogue. His father bathed in the river daily, far into the winter, and scorned a fire in his study. Thring used to tell how pleased the sons were on the few occasions when they could score off him. It was not often they could, but he told us with some glee how on coming into the study for morning prayers, his brother Henry was rubbing his hands, and saying how cold it was, when the old gentleman sharply asked: "What's cold?" The servants just then filed in. "Ice," said Henry, and all knelt at once, which prevented a rejoinder, but gave the family something to chuckle over for a long time.

His father came to see Edward at Uppingham, about the year 1860, and, as was his invariable custom, he rode from Somersetshire on horseback, with a groom in attendance to look after his horse and the small valise which was all the luggage he allowed himself. He obtained a half-holiday for the school and, as one little boy was out of school with some minor ailment, and was sitting by Thring's patent fire grate,[1] he in the study

[1] *Vide infra.*

sympathised with him for not sharing the holiday, and gave him five shillings in compensation.

Of his mother Thring was devotedly fond, and never spoke of her without lowering his voice. He prided himself on being always a dutiful son, but he once told me that for all that, the two greatest events of his life were done contrary to their wishes, his taking Uppingham, and his marriage. This latter he never for a moment regretted. His wife's mother, a grand old lady of remarkable character and proved courage, lived with them for the rest of her days, and his sister-in-law, coming to the school-house when the children were quite young, remained with them all her life, and was a great help to the family and a very kind friend to many generations of school-boys, who called her " Aunt Anna," just as they called the Headmaster by the affectionate name of " Teddy."

Next to his courage and energy, I think that the most prominent trait in his nature was his love of children, and his sympathy and gentleness in dealing with his boys. Personally he was always most friendly to me. I had been to no private school, and was the youngest boy in his house. Thring, who did all the work with his sixth form, and looked over all their composition, also attended himself to all housemaster's duties, always dining with us and saying with resonant and earnest voice the Latin grace of some thirty words, which, thanks to Mr Owen, has now been reintroduced in the School-house.

After lock-up, when we retired each to his own study, he would frequently come round and look in on each of us, and have a word or two with most. Then at nine he read prayers to the House, and at ten-fifteen punctually he came round the dormitories and with "Good-night to you!" turned out the gas. This ended his day. He had been in school by 7 a.m., and he now went off to bed, and slept soundly all the night. Before he had built a school hospital and got a trained Matron living in it, if one of us was ailing, we had to stay in bed in our cubicle till allowed to get up and come down to the "sick-room." I had to stay in bed in my first term for a fortnight, and the Headmaster, whose day was so full of necessary work, used every other day to come up and sit on my bed and talk of home and encourage me to learn Macaulay's Lays by heart, always quoting his favourite passage with gusto :

> " And wounded horses kicking,
> And snorting purple foam,
> Right well did such a couch befit
> A Consular of Rome."

Nearly twenty years later we find him going to one of the " Hill Houses " (for four of the best houses were built about a quarter of a mile from the chapel and schoolrooms, on the hilly Rockingham Road) in order to comfort the Captain of the School, who had broken down from overwork. His Diary has the following, dated June, 1874 :

" It is curious how one's trials turn into blessings. I was able not only to feel with him and give him sound advice through my own sufferings and weakness, but still more to make him feel, I think, quite differently when he found how much I had had of the same kind. He said : ' I always thought you had an iron constitution.' I answered : ' Indeed, no, for seventeen years here I never had a perfect day of health, and I owe, under God, my sitting here alive by you to-day to the care in diet and exercise I have taken, ever since I went to Cambridge.'" A week later, the diary says: "After dining yesterday I walked round the houses and gardens with a Mr Greenfield, and saw a most marvellous proof of our school tone which he observed first—a number of ripe strawberries bordering the boys' path to R——'s House, untouched and safe. The more remarkable, because it is not only the path for his own boys, but for his class and the school generally. When I recollect my own school-life, it is astonishing."

The following is the same kind of thing in a minor degree. We had an Etonian as master, and he and I, having as yet no houses of our own, both had our classes in the big schoolroom; for each housemaster took his class in the dining-hall of his own house; classrooms, except for the sixth form, not having been built till fifty years later, under the present Headmaster, Rev. R. H. Owen. Now one day Mr G. said to me, with some astonishment on his face: "Do you know, I asked a boy the way this morning, *and he told me!*" "Well," I said, "what did you

EDWARD THRING

expect?" "I don't quite know; but I do know that when I was at school, if a master asked a boy the way, he would have misdirected him as a matter of course." This struck me, who knew no school but Uppingham, as a very curious state of things.

Because Thring was tender-hearted, and sympathetic to an unusual degree, I do not mean to say that he had not his fierce moments, when he pitched into us in terrific style, pouring his strong vocabulary in undisguised scorn upon our devoted heads.

A sense of humour is salvation to many a man, and how well it served Thring is illustrated by the following :

One day he had been pitching into the school for what he regarded as a lapse from the principles of " true life " ; somebody had done something mean and untruthful, and he poured out his wrath on the whole school ; then, as he was leaving the schoolroom, there arose a not very marked hiss, a thing never heard by him before or after. He turned at the entrance and with a grim smile said to the boys—" There are but two things that make that noise. Geese and snakes, you can take your choice, gentlemen." The school saw that " Teddy " had scored ; and the smile broadened on his countenance as he heard " Three cheers for Mr Thring," which was at once responded to unanimously, only to be smothered in hearty laughter. Thring knew his boys so well that he was not afraid at times to chaff them.

I must admit that he was a terror to any class, below the sixth, that had to go up to him with a construing lesson. We sometimes got through safely, but the funk that he established in all our bosoms was enough to last a life-time. I have, ever since those days, firmly believed that every *great* Headmaster has a superhuman power of terrifying a boy.

Perhaps the best instance of this terrifying power is afforded by this story of the Great Duke of Wellington, whom no one could accuse of want of courage, and Dr Keate, of Eton, in whose small body Kinglake tells us there was the pluck of ten battalions. I once told Gladstone, who was telling me about his time at Eton, that I had

EDWARD THRING

known Keate, and Gladstone turned half round in his chair at dinner and said : " Well, if you say you knew Keate, I must believe you, but I should not have thought it possible." But he was forgetting that the Doctor had lived for thirteen years at Hartley Wespall, after he had retired from Eton and that, as my father was curate of Hartley, I got to know Dr Keate and the charming Mrs Keate, and their son, Johnny, and three of the daughters. There was nothing terrible about the Dr then, and my memory of him (I was a very small boy at the time) is of a kind little old gentleman, in a black tailed coat, playing cricket on the lawn with his wife and daughters.

But he was a different man among the boys at Eton. So, when the Duke told some friends at his Club that he was going to Eton next day to confess to Keate that he was the boy who had defaced some statue, with red paint I think, and the culprit had never confessed, in spite of Keate's kindly promise that if the boy came forward, he would give him as sound a flogging as he had ever had and was likely to have in his life, the Duke's friends said : " You don't mean to say you are going to do that?" "Yes, I do." "Then please come in here afterwards and tell us all about it." He promised, and when they met him,

"How did you get on?" they said.

"Well, it was not quite what I expected; for a long time I could not get a chance to speak about it, but I got him at last to a window recess and said, 'You remember that statue which was defaced, and no one knew by whom?' 'Yes, do you know anything about it?' 'No, sir.'"

"You do not mean to say you said that?"

"Yes, I do; and I mean to say that if any one of you had been in my place you would have said the same."

It would seem that, whether Dukes or peasants, all boys alike have the same feelings towards their master if the latter is really efficient and follows Solomon's precept, for only a short time ago I read, in a Suffolk church, an epitaph on a Westmorland man, who " was eleven years the beloved schoolmaster of this town, and then unfortunately shott, 23 of November, 1723, aged 32."

"Profuit et placuit, miscebat et utile dulci,
Discipulis terror, deliciæ que suis."

EDWARD THRING

As I read this, I thought of those construing lessons when we were " up to Teddy." But his kind heart was always able to dispel this magisterial ferocity. How often have I seen him calling in boys from the quad. to his garden, and shaking his well-laden plum trees for them to fill their pockets, or carrying one or two small boys off to his tiny dining-room, where Mrs Thring always had a magnificent sort of wedding cake on the sideboard, and cutting off a huge chunk for us to carry off to our studies, and as I shared a study with a bosom friend, Thring always added a second huge wedge, " For the bosom."

It is sad to think that on top of all the disheartening conduct of his governors, he should have had such constant physical ill-health and pain, which led him at last to long to leave Uppingham, a thing which we thought, after all its prosperity and evident success, he would never wish to do, but he never distressed us by letting us into the secret of his suffering. Moreover, his intensely religious faith which made him see God in all the happenings of life, kept him going ; and when the holidays came, he gave himself up to enjoy to the full the beauties of Nature, and the loving hearts of his children and his boys. Now and then he was, indeed, asked by one or two of his masters to take half a day's holiday in term time. I took him once to see Crowland Abbey, and he said to me : " Now this is what I like, to be taken about, and for you to order the trap, and to get my ticket, and arrange everything for me, and leave me nothing to do, but to do as I am told, and enjoy all I see."

The disclosures of his diary, on which Parkin had to draw so largely in writing his life, were a shock to all of us. That the debt he had been obliged to incur had been such a life-long burden, and that he had, as he said, failed to get all his masters to fully understand his principles, and feared, lest, when he left it, the school would not carry on as he had intended, these were the fears and sorrows that were to him so heart-breaking ; but he did not lose his native courage, and happily most of his masters came to trust him fully in the end, and the boys, with very few exceptions, nobly responded to his teaching and training, so that his heart found much to rejoice in.

EDWARD THRING

Being a hero-worshipper, Thring, in spite of the dismal entries in his diary, and his constant want of money which was absolutely essential, when everything had to be built before he could offer a living wage to his masters, was an optimist. He seized with much heartfelt joy on every sign of what he called " true life " among his boys, and gave God thanks for it. I can never forget the real delight with which, after having prayers in his own house, he came up to one of the hill-houses to give his grateful thanks to the boys, " for their zeal in clearing themselves and the school from cribs and dishonest work." He notes in his diary that it had been " An infinite pleasure to me," as it certainly was to the house he was addressing, " It is a great onward step. The being able to praise, is the battle won ; and never before have all ranks in a house worked so well together for truth."

This was due to what Gladstone called *the system*. The præposters in the house had done it all without any consultation with the housemaster, and they were no prigs, but had the respect and ready assistance of all the house, and the result of their work remained ; there was no looking back. The note made by the housemaster was, " The proudest day of my life."

How well he laid the foundation of his school has been seen, and he kept it all going till the gradual giving way of his health and strength loosened somewhat his grip on the tiller, and his successor found a good deal to do in keying up the machine which should have been acting automatically. He always insisted that the two main facts on which the school was built up were, first, the individual attention which every boy, clever or stupid, *must* have paid to him, and secondly, the provision of the proper *machinery* and proper tools for training each boy, and he added that nothing that could be done by " machinery " should be left for men to do.

His fight for the religious character of the school was a necessity of his nature, one of his deepest convictions being that it was " hopeless to think of a first-rate school in which the Headmaster within his own scope had not free and powerful religious influences to bring to bear."

EDWARD THRING

Thring had given the school a holiday when the numbers reached 100, the præpostors had claimed one for 200, and again for 300 (Thring's proposed limit) in August, 1865. Indeed, the school was quite full in October, 1864, from which date boys had to be refused. Thus the numbers rose from 50 to 300 in ten years, in spite of the Jackson set-back in 1861-2.

It was this principle of limiting the numbers of the school and consequently the numbers in each of the eleven houses that was the main grievance of the housemasters. For all knew that it was the last few boys that made a house pay.

"Every boy is good for something" was an article of Thring's creed. "If he can't write Iambics or excel in Latin prose, he has at least eyes and hands and ears. Turn him into the carpenter's shop, make him a botanist or a chemist, encourage him to express himself in music, and if he fails all round, here at least he shall learn to read in public his mother tongue and write thoughtfully an English essay."

It is impossible to exaggerate the great importance he had always attached to the teaching of

EDWARD THRING

English (which, along with drawing, he made compulsory through all the lower forms), and the teaching throughout the whole school of the art of reading aloud. This is a thing for which many of the Sixth Form have never ceased to bless his memory. Each year for a couple of days the whole school was assembled to be taught elocution by the Rev A. J. D'Orsey, a master in his profession, and every boy put through his paces, the trials lasting through every school-hour of the day ; and certainly we did learn the art of reading aloud both prose and poetry, in a very marked degree. " To teach boys the grammar or common-sense rules of their own language, and to make them all analyse the sentences they read," was one of Thring's chief aims in the lower and middle forms, and he wrote a book on *The Principles of Grammar*, and one on *Grammatical Analysis*, which are monuments of his industry, gave one some ideas, and were as useful to the teachers as to the pupils. But I think they added a new terror to the Thursday afternoons when the Headmaster took the upper forms nominally in a classical lesson.

English is made much more of now in all schools than it was 50 years ago—and if only Headmasters were as bold as Thring was, to put new ideas on a practical basis, the " teaching by the humanities," that is to say by giving pupils plenty of the best English literature to read, in school and out, which was the method of that wonderful educationalist, Miss Charlotte Mason, might work similar wonders to those which can be seen and tested in some hundred and fifty elementary schools at the present moment, notably in the West Riding and in Gloucestershire, where his method is widely practised.

Our masters at Uppingham were, in Thring's first three lustra, not a very literary set. But I must mention with never-failing gratitude, the Rev Duncan Matthias, master of the Upper Vth, who introduced us to Charles Lamb, and started several of us in the lifelong pursuit of the best in English literature.

In the VIth Thring daily made us see the beauty and poetry of Nature. He was a Wordsworthian, and aimed at making us observe and think, and encouraged us to learn by heart from the classics both verse and prose, and choice passages from the greatest of the English poets.

In October, 1876, two fatalities from typhoid in the Preparatory School made everyone most anxious, and, in order to put things right, the school was dismissed in November, to return in January. In December, the masters had got the best advice, and had all the school-houses examined; and though they were all found to be in good order, every least suggestion of the Nottingham Borough Engineer was at once carried out. But the mischief was in the town, and though the whole body of masters had sent a memorial to the Guardians, asking for analysis of the water and inspection of the town sewers, no steps were taken by the town, and the Governors took no notice whatever. We fondly hoped that the local Sanitary Authorities would bestir themselves, but all that their Sanitary Inspector did was to pronounce two of the wells perfectly pure, which the London analyst in a day or two flatly condemned. But still the Governors could see no need for going beyond the local authority.

Upon this, Thring and the masters appealed

to the Central Authority in London. The Government Engineer decided that the local Sanitary Board must deal with this work at once, otherwise the Central Board would send down men to do it, and charge it on the parish. The Government's kind help was a strong contrast to the sulky resistance of the local people. But the greatest assistance was that of the Liverpool and Manchester Trustees, Messrs Jacob and Birley, backed up by the Hereditary Patron, Mr A. C. Johnson. In January, 1876, the school returned, but the town had done little to remedy the bad state of the drains. Deaths kept occurring in the town, but it was not till the Chairman of the local Sanitary Board had died of fever, that the work of cleansing the town, and remaking its inexpressibly bad main sewers, was taken in hand.

Meantime it became clear, as fresh cases developed, that the school could not stay at Uppingham, and no parents would return their boys a second time to an infected place; for in March the school was again dismissed. And now the idea of migrating was caught hold of by

Thring, and no sooner broached, than he decided to carry it out.

The lesson of the day read by Thring in chapel on the last Sunday and the day before he started to look for a haven of refuge for the exiled school, had in it this verse : " Behold I am with thee and will keep thee in all places whithersoever thou goest " (*Gen.* 28, 15), and in that faith he went forth undoubting. But first of all a place of sanctuary had to be found, big enough to hold us all. Masters went various ways to find it, the best place being judged on inspection to be Borth, near Aberystwith on the Bay of Cardigan. Thither eighteen truckloads of beds and bedding, etc., were despatched from Uppingham, and unloaded on the Borth platform of the Cambrian Railway, before the end of March. All the goods were sorted and taken to the fourteen houses which formed the street from the station to The Beach. Masters spent many strenuous hours in carrying bedsteads and putting them up. The big hotel on the sea front was arranged to take 150 boys, with the Headmaster's family, and two Matrons, and a master to look after the boys ; and dining accommodation was provided for two hundred more, for the school all messed together. A wooden schoolroom to hold all the school was built, rooms in cottages secured to serve as studies, everything in short which was needed for carrying on the school was ready by the time a long train poured out on April 4th, 1876, nearly three hundred boys to take up their interrupted school life at " Uppingham by the Sea."

And all this, from the time they decided to leave their Midland home, the finding of the place, adapting it, furnishing it, and getting into the new quarters, was the work of but three weeks. Thring had saved the school. This thought, and his freedom from the local worries, and the fine sea air and bright surroundings on the Welsh coast, and the having it all to ourselves, were a paradise to him. All the boys but one or two turned up, and as the year of exile advanced, the entries at Borth exceeded the leavings.

The school found a good friend in Sir Pryse Pryse, of Gogerddan, who gave us the use of a meadow, which the big school roller, transported to Wales, soon reduced to a fairly good cricket-ground; he also allowed us to fish in his stream, and brought his harriers twice a week for the boys to follow. Every one was out of doors as much as possible, and instead of a bell, which could not be heard for the noise of the sea, a flag flying in front of the hotel was dipped to recall them when the hour for meals or school arrived. These Borth flags, three in all, hang now at the back of the seated statue of the great Headmaster at the west end of the Uppingham School chapel, lit by an electric light, and close to the beautiful annexe which has been designed and built by Mr Newton, himself an " old boy," as a memorial to those, more than four hundred in number, who gave their lives for King and country in the Great War.

At the present time it is beginning to be felt that cricket and football do not quite supply all that the mind and the imagination of a boy at school requires. The search for flowers and ferns, the collecting of moths and butterflies, and the study of the habits of birds, all help to enlarge the mind, and to encourage habits of observation. At Borth all this was possible, and there were also sea shells, a great variety of bright-coloured pebbles, and all the wonderful sea things which boys could find in the rock-pools and creeks ; and then the excursions to the mountains and to the beautiful waterfalls were a new and never-failing delight ; and by the time that a full year had passed, and the school went home for its Easter holidays in 1877, their parents found the boys so grown, from their out-of-door life in that healthy air, that all their trousers needed lengthening.

When first the Governors gave leave for the school to migrate, one of them, with native discourtesy, said that they only knew the school at Uppingham ; whilst it was away they knew, and wished to know, nothing of it. At the end of the first term, without medical authority, the Governors ordered the school back. Thring refused to come unless the town was officially certified to be clean and healthy. This certificate the local authorities were quite ready to give, but the Government officials refused, and told Thring on no account to think of returning for some time

EDWARD THRING

to come. So another term was spent on the Cardigan coast, and we learnt what wind on the west coast could be. In our houses, when the street door was opened, the carpets blew up in every room, or, as Keats puts it, " The carpets rose along the gusty floor."

Even after Christmas the slow Midlanders had not finished the business, and again we had to return to our haven in the west, only getting to our houses at Uppingham after the Easter holidays, by which time one-third of the whole school came to an Uppingham they had never seen before.

Two or three instances of difficulties quickly overcome may be mentioned here. When first migration was mooted, an old boy[1] gave up his appointment as House Surgeon in a big London hospital, and offered to take the post of sanitary officer for the stricken school. His offer was welcomed, and he was soon hard at work at Borth. Then, to the dismay of many, we quickly had an outbreak of scarlet fever. An isolated house was formed to serve as a hospital, it was newly built and had neither doors nor windows,

[1] Dr Christopher Childs.

only the frames for the latter. The Sanitary Officer and another old-boy master, who had learnt in the school carpenter's shop, set to work and made them in one day, and at 11 p.m. the splendid hospital nurse whom we had brought from Uppingham, was on her knees scrubbing the floor, and the next day the patients were in. Happily the outbreak was soon quelled, and never reappeared. Another time a cry arose for more studies. " How many do you want ? " asked the Headmaster. " Five and twenty ? Well, I'll get them." He set off, and in a short time was back with : " That is all right ; I have got them ; they will be ready for use to-morrow."

The inhabitants, especially the cottagers, could deny him nothing, and when we left, they all turned out to address him, and lament our departure, singling out for special thanks the Headmaster and the Sanitary Officer, who had attended their children when sick, and refused all fees. The Welsh may not be dependable for statement of facts, but their gratitude for kindness is genuine and almost overwhelming. One day Borth will long remember, when a high tide swept away their low and loose-built sea-wall, and flooded the little street. Thring turned the whole school out on to the beach to bring in big stones, and got the wall replaced in a day.

The return from exile to home quarters was easy, and the magnificent welcome from the little town, now drained and free from pestilence, took us all by surprise. We passed from station to schoolroom under arches of greenery and strings of flags, and a warm address of welcome by the leading townsmen produced a happy speech from Thring, and from thenceforth, the town and the school worked and walked together as friends.

Thring made a great attempt after this to elevate the taste in music and literature of the townsfolk, through the Mutual Improvement Society. But they were not so easy to impress as his boys were.

His removal of the school bodily, when threatened with extinction, brought him the heartiest letters of congratulation from many a headmaster, and from countless others. Certainly it saved the school, and at the first yearly commemoration of the great exodus, Thring ended one of his sermons with, " The school died, and is alive again. Do not betray that life."

Among other things, Thring was a poet. He wrote the Uppingham School Songs, which have a splendid go in them, and many lyrics of considerable merit. In one of his *Borth Lyrics* he says :

> " Never, oh never, was heard before
> That a school as old as an old oak tree,
> Fast by the roots was flung up in the air
> And pitched on its feet by the sea, the sea,
> Pitched on its feet by the sea."

Such was the wonderful achievement of Uppingham's great re-founder, and all headmasters at the time agreed that there was not another man in England who could have done it. After the return, Thring founded one more enterprise. It was his desire to see Uppingham boys on leaving the school keep open hearts and ready hands to help one another in all good works, hence the birth of the *Uppingham School Society*, which, since 1879, has each year given generous assistance to " any old Uppingham boy or master in any good public work which he may have in hand."

EDWARD THRING

1884 saw the celebration of the tercentenary of the old foundation. 1887, his last year of life, had brought the Headmistresses of the great girls' schools and colleges to his house and garden for two of the happiest days of his working life. On Saturday, October 15th, he read the last verse of the Psalms at his schoolhouse evening prayers with his usual impressiveness : " So he fed them with a faithful and true heart, and ruled them prudently with all his power."

Next Sunday he was reading the Communion office in Chapel, but after the Collect he resigned the book and, refusing assistance, walked past all the rows of wondering boys, down the nave and out of the Chapel, and his school saw him no more. He had his prayer, " Work to the end of my life," granted. The sermon he was to have preached that afternoon was ready on his study table. He inquired on Tuesday : " Is work going on all right ? " and, on the assurance given, said : " That's good."

The inflammation of the lungs, after this, rapidly increased, and before the week was out he passed away.

The *Spectator* of October 29th had this sentence in its notice of him : " If ever a man of prayer moved boys and men alike to a sense of noble endeavour, it was Edward Thring."

On October 27th, borne by eight of his masters and old boys, and followed by a long train of sorrowing pupils, past and present, he was laid to rest in the old churchyard.

Thring was gone, but his work goes on, and by the courage and skill of his successors, while the spirit remains the same, the surroundings have been greatly improved. In earlier days, when Thring asked the Governors that some of the money which his continually growing numbers had brought to their coffers, should be spent on the buildings necessary for their use, their reply was to spend a lot of Uppingham money on new buildings at Oakham. Now the money was to be directed to its proper channel, and Dr Selwyn, late principal of Liverpool College, soon had a new school house, while the dormitories and offices, along with Thring's diminutive study in the old hospital, were turned into a beautiful library. Science rooms and a lecture hall were built, and an entrance gateway and tower added, and a gallery was put up at the west end of the Chapel, under which the fine seated statue of the founder of the present school is placed. A new Memorial Hall to those who fell in the Boer War, so made as to do duty, in the first place, as a gymnasium, was opened by Lord Roberts, and inaugurated for occasional use as a concert hall, in honour of Mr David, by Dr Joachim. In Dr Selwyn's time, too, a new and efficient water-supply was obtained from a distance, at a cost of £18,000, and the Rifle Corps started, and an edict passed that every boy in the school must learn to use the rifle, a splendid innovation, which has borne good fruit.

After' twenty years, Dr Selwyn gave place to Durham's Headmaster, Rev. H. W. McKenzie, who got new music schools built and, with help from an old boy, doubled the Museum accommodation, and, greatest feat of all, managed, with the whole-hearted aid of the Rector, Archdeacon Moore, to get the trustees to buy a fine tract of grass-land of some 35 acres, which was in danger of being purchased by an ironstone Company,

EDWARD THRING

who would have mined it right up to the edge of our Hill-houses. Most of this was then laid down at a cost of £5,000, by the generosity of another old boy, as a magnificent cricket-field. This field is one of the chief glories of Uppingham. A few years later the Rev. R. H. Owen succeeded to the Headmastership. Under him Mr Newton's beautiful annexe, as a memorial to those who fell in the Great War, has been added to the Chapel, classrooms for the whole school have been put up, and the Great Hall, a truly magnificent building, as a War Memorial, added to the group of Street's buildings, his schoolroom being turned into a School Museum ; also a new pavilion has been given by Mr W. S. Patterson and the widow of C. E. Green, in which will be a tribute to the school's finest cricketer, A. P. Lucas.

Thring's best-known book is *The Theory and Practice of Teaching*, published in 1883, with a second edition in 1885. His principles of education, viz., that no boy should be sent away because he does not get on fast enough, and that something to attract and hold every individual should be supplied by a perfect school, are everlasting. He told a newly-appointed master that he must never consider his work ended, if he could get on a stupid or backward boy by more. His great aim to make every boy think, and also use his eyes as well as his brain, will probably become the aim of all teachers in time.

"Remember that in no case can nonsense ever be right," was his warning before setting an examination paper. He was fond of the *Book of Proverbs*, and was the author of many maxims himself, such as "Never be doing nothing, either work or play or sleep ; never combine two of these," " If you don't do small things well, you'll never do great things at all," " Know what you know," " The trained mind is worth all the knowledge in the world."

His most remarkable lesson, and the one which made one think, and gave one new ideas, more than any lesson or lecture we ever had, was his morning Bible lesson. R. L. Nettleship used to say that he got more from that half hour, than from any other lesson, and I have heard the same many times. One of his most famous pupils writes :
" In his Divinity lesson he took the Hebrew heroes

and made them living men before us, and translated the New Testament into modern times.

"But it was difficult, because he took for granted that we were following his train of thought, which it often took us some time to pick up, but when he saw that we were puzzled, he always helped us, and it was seldom that we went away without something solid, and of real value, to chew upon, for ' he taught as one that had authority, and not as the scribes.' "

To his old pupils he was a very great man, great in conception and in invention (he invented a smoke-consuming grate, and used it in his study, and wrote to my father thirteen good reasons why it was the best in the world), great in perseverance in the face of opposition, great in organisation, great in courage, and great in character. Mr Parking told me that the Governor of the N.W. Provinces once said to him, " I have known all the great men who have made their mark in India, Lawrence, Edwards, Nicholson, Dufferin, and other famous men in England, but it is only when I have had a walk and talk with Edward Thring that I have had the feeling that I have

EDWARD THRING

been with a very great man," and Parking said he could quite understand it.

His constant aim to make boys think, especially before they wrote anything in an examination, he used often to emphasise by telling the story of the man who asked W. Opie, the painter, " What do you mix your colours with ? " and received the answer, " With brains, sir."

The pupil who best understood Thring was Dr J. H. Skrine, who, after winning a scholarship at Corpus (the Newdigate) and a fellowship at Merton, came back to Uppingham as a master, and remained for fourteen years the constant companion of his old Headmaster to the end, when he became Warden of Glenalmond, and besides several volumes of poetry wrote the history of Borth in a volume called " Uppingham by the Sea." He was the truest friend, and the most generous that I ever knew, and his beautiful book, *A Memory of Edward Thring*, is the best guide to the history of the re-founding of Uppingham, and the methods and characteristics of its founder. Thring himself made no boast of his great work. He said he was organising a system which any set of people with reasonable ability and honest intentions could carry out ; " I am only a sower, let others reap " ; but he felt, with some sadness and sense of failure, that a good deal that he had personally contributed to the work would not go on. I believe that here he was undervaluing the deep impress of his personality on many generations of boys.

" Only consider," says Mr Skrine, " what it means to have sent out, and every year for the space of a generation, a group of young men protected in a signal degree from boyhood's disasters, and steadied against those of manhood by the principles which a moral genius had stamped upon them, and think what praise it is to say of a worker at the long day's end, that, save for losses beyond human love and diligence to recover, of all that have been given him, he has lost none . . . certainly, on the evils of public school life he laid a stronger hand than anyone in his generation."

In 1825 a new portrait of Thring was painted by Mr Lance Calkin, which is an excellent likeness, and hangs in the Great Hall along with those of Paul David, Dr Selwyn, and Rev. H. W. McKenzie. This is a great gain to the school, for the portrait which we had before was a very poor one. It wanted what artists call a bit more " devil " in it.

The last great work of the present Headmaster is the raising of a fund for the purchase of the school houses, some of which are still private property. He has also put up a Table of names of school benefactors, in the Great Hall, which is, we rejoice to see, getting filled up with the names of Thring's old pupils as donors.

For Product Safety Concerns and Information please contact our EU
representative GPSR@taylorandfrancis.com
Taylor & Francis Verlag GmbH, Kaufingerstraße 24, 80331 München, Germany

www.ingramcontent.com/pod-product-compliance
Lightning Source LLC
Chambersburg PA
CBHW070542300426
44113CB00011B/1760